汉语桥-中学生夏令营
Chinese Bridge Summer Camp for Foreign Students

中国欢迎你 Welcome to China 短期汉语系列教材

孔子学院总部/国家汉办
Confucius Institute Headquarters(Hanban)

Xue Shufa Shuimohua

学书法·水墨画

Chinese Calligraphy and Ink Painting

修订版 Revised Edition

才艺类

高等教育出版社·北京

“中国欢迎你”短期汉语系列教材

总策划 许　琳

总监制 王永利

策　划 陈　默　邵亦鹏

监　制 梁　宇　薛　佼

前言

为帮助“汉语桥—夏/冬令营”学生以及所有对中国感兴趣的外国朋友在较短时间内了解中国的语言与文化、历史与风俗，孔子学院总部/国家汉办组织研发，高等教育出版社于2011年正式出版发行了“中国欢迎你”短期汉语系列教材，受到了海内外教师和学生的普遍认可和喜爱。

为顺应汉语教学与文化体验项目的不断发展，孔子学院总部/国家汉办对教材使用情况开展了调研，编写组由此获得了教师和学生们对教材的宝贵反馈意见，对“中国欢迎你”短期汉语系列教材进行了系统修订和完善，精心研制并推出修订版。

◉ 适用对象

本系列教材主要适用于来华参加夏/冬令营的学生，海外孔子学院和孔子课堂也可将其用作教学辅助资源。

◉ 教材构成

本系列教材分为三大类：语言类、才艺类和地域类。

《学书法·水墨画》是才艺类教材中的一册，主要内容包括中国书法和水墨画工具、汉字与书法、书体与书法、水墨画等。本书将文化与才艺学习有机地结合起来，同时配以丰富的练习和活动，目的在于帮助学习者在较短时间内了解中国书法和水墨画的基本知识，掌握基本的书写和绘画技能。本书的参考教学时间为6～8学时。

◉ 编写特色

1. 适用性：充分考虑海外青少年学习者短期学习的学习特点，以学习者为中心，合理设计教学内容和教学顺序，用深入浅出、图文并茂的方式展示汉语与文化。

2. 活动式：以任务和活动为主线，寓教于乐，注重实效，便于教师进行教学设计，充分调动学习者的学习兴趣，实现轻松有效的课堂教学。

3. 资源性：为教师和学习者提供各类丰富的素材，以及各类可以直接动手操作的练习，满足学习者的个性化需求。

让我们翻开书，一起去感知充满魅力的汉语和中国文化！

编委会

2016年2月

Contents 目 录

Chinese Calligraphy and Ink Painting

书法·水墨画

Tools of Chinese Calligraphy and Ink Painting
书画工具

The unique charm and elegance of Chinese calligraphy and painting would be impossible without these crucial writing tools.

中国书法和水墨画之所以呈现出独特的魅力，离不开其主要的书画工具。

The brush, ink, paper and inkstone, often called the *wenfang sibao* 文房四宝 (four treasures of the study), are unique to Chinese calligraphy, and in ancient China would have been an indispensable part of the life of the scholar.

笔、墨、纸、砚是中国独有的文字书写工具，被称为“文房四宝”，是中国古代文人生活中不可缺少的一部分。

笔 Brush: a paintbrush traditionally made from bamboo and animal hair.
bǐ 毛笔，用竹管和动物毛发做成。

墨 Ink: either liquid ink or an inkstick.
mò 墨汁或墨块。

纸 Paper: meaning *xuan* paper, a type of light, portable and easily stored paper.
zhǐ 指宣纸，轻便、易保存。

砚 Inkstone: a tool for grinding ink.
yàn 研墨的工具。

Let's Try 试一试

Try to write some characters or to paint on *xuan* paper and on an ordinary piece of paper respectively with brush. Can you feel the difference?

用毛笔分别在宣纸上和我们平时用的白纸上写字、画画，感觉一下有什么不同。

Chinese Characters and Calligraphy
汉字与书法

Chinese characters are one of the most ancient forms of writing in the world. Chinese calligraphy is the art of writing Chinese characters. To make their writing neater and more aesthetically pleasing, people often practice writing characters in square grids, a custom which led to the formation of the rules of Chinese calligraphy, also giving rise to the epithet "square script" on account of the unique method of practicing.

汉字是世界上最古老的文字之一。书法是汉字书写的艺术。人们为了把字写得整齐美观，就在方格内练字，这种习惯逐渐形成了汉字的书写规范，汉字也由此被称为“方块字”。

Chinese characters are comprised of strokes and components. The stroke is the smallest unit within a character. The component is made up of strokes and can be written independently as characters.

组成汉字的结构单位有笔画和部件。笔画是汉字的最小构成单位。部件是由笔画构成的可以独立书写的组字单位。

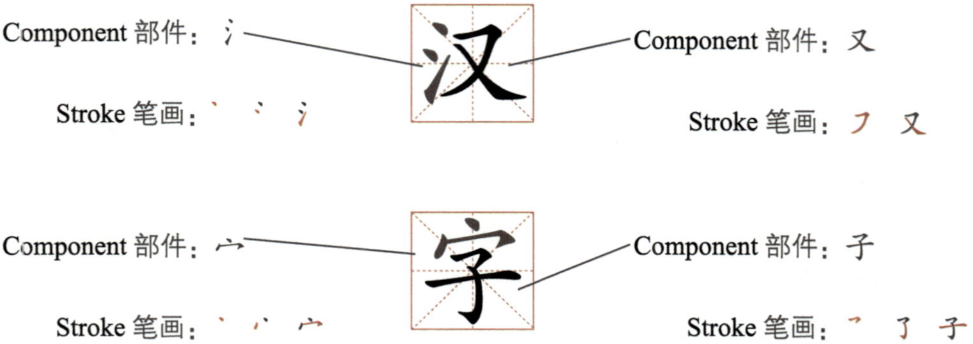

Chinese characters can be divided into two main types: *dutizi* **独体字** (single characters) and *hetizi* **合体字** (compound characters). Single characters are directly made up of a small number of strokes, difficult to break down into smaller parts, and relatively complete and independent. Compound characters are comprised of two or more components and can be categorized by their differing structures. When writing compound characters, attention should be paid to keeping the various components tightly aligned, for the sake of both accuracy and aesthetic appearance.

汉字可以分成独体字和合体字两种。独体字是指以笔画为直接单位构成的汉字。独体字不易拆分，相对完整而独立。合体字是指那些由两个或两个以上部件构成的汉字。合体字有不同的结构类型，书写合体字时应该将各个部件写得紧凑些，这既是为了书写准确，也是为了美观。

独体字				合体字			
也 ●	月 ●	身 ●	中 ●	他 ◐	朋 ◐	忠 ⊖	谢 ◍
土 ●	日 ●	果 ●	斤 ●	晶 ∴	裹 ⊜	近 ◟	国 ⊙

Let's Think 想一想

Put the following characters into categories according to their structures.
根据汉字结构为下列汉字归类。

① 也	② 是	③ 月	④ 因	⑤ 他	⑥ 忠
⑦ 朋	⑧ 花	⑨ 园	⑩ 中	⑪ 回	⑫ 对

● ☐ ☐ ☐ ◐ ☐ ☐ ☐

⊖ ☐ ☐ ☐ ⊙ ☐ ☐ ☐

Each Chinese characters have a particular number of strokes, from as few as one to dozens of individual strokes. The strokes have a prescribed order, known as the *bishun* 笔顺 (stroke order), which must be followed when writing. For example, first horizontal and then vertical, first left-falling stroke, then right-falling stroke, first the middle and then the sides, etc.

不同汉字的笔画有少有多，从一画到几十画不等。汉字笔画书写起来有一定的顺序，这就是“笔顺”，如“从左到右，从上到下，先中间后两边”等。

Let's Try 试一试

Write out the stroke order for these characters.
写出下列汉字的笔顺。

中 丨 冂 口 中

国

书

法

Answers 答案

第3页

- ● 也 月 中
- ◐ 他 明 对
- ⊖ 是 忠 花
- ⊙ 因 园 回

Styles of Chinese Calligraphy Scripts
书体与书法

The evolution of Chinese characters can be divided into several stages: oracle bone script, bronze script, small seal script, clerical script, regular script, cursive script, and running script. Among them, seal, clerical, regular, cursive, and running script now form the five main writing styles used in China, and are known in Chinese as the "Big Five" script styles.

汉字的演变过程可分为甲骨文、金文、小篆、隶书、楷书、草书、行书几个阶段。其中“篆、隶、楷、草、行”是中国文字的主要书写形式，被称为五大类书体。

①甲骨文 Jiǎgǔwén Oracle bone script
②金　文 Jīnwén Bronze script
③小　篆 Xiǎozhuàn Small seal script
④隶　书 Lìshū Clerical script
⑤楷　书 Kǎishū Regular script
⑥草　书 Cǎoshū Cursive script
⑦行　书 Xíngshū Running script

Oracle bone script 甲骨文

Over 3000 years ago, in the ancient Shang and Zhou Dynasty, people in ancient China used inscriptions on turtle shells and animal bones to divine the future. The script was given the Chinese name *jiaguwen* 甲骨文 literally meaning "script on shell and bone" due to the unique nature of their medium.

在距今3000多年前的中国商周时代，人们把关于占卜的文字刻写在龟类和兽类的甲、骨上，被后人发现后，被命名为"甲骨文"。

Oracle bone script is a kind of seal script, which is held to be the most ancient form of Chinese writing. Its characteristics include very thin strokes with many straight lines and squared edges, characters can often be written in several different ways.

甲骨文是篆书的一种，被看作是"最古老的汉字"。它的特点是笔道细、直笔多、转折处多为方形，一个字往往有多种写法。

Let's Think 想一想

Match the oracle bone script characters with the modern Chinese meaning by drawing lines between the two characters.

根据甲骨文的字形，将其和现代汉字连线。

山(shān) 瓜(guā) 水(shuǐ) 牛(niú)

Let's Try 试一试

Re-write the following characters in oracle bone script.
摹写下列汉字的甲骨文。

1. sun 日（rì）/ moon 月（yuè）

2. mountain 山（shān）/ water 水（shuǐ）

3. cow 牛 (niú) / sheep 羊 (yáng)

4. dragon 龙 (lóng) / phoenix 凤 (fèng)

Small seal　小篆

Small seal script is one kind of seal script. In the year 221 BCE *Qin Shihuang* 秦始皇 (the First Emperor of China) united China, at the same time unifying the different forms of Chinese characters into one, now known as "small seal script". This style of script is characterized by its symmetry, with many characters displaying not only horizontal and vertical symmetry, but internal symmetry between individual components within the character. In addition, the strokes of small seal characters have smooth curves and an even length and thickness.

小篆也是篆书的一种。公元前221年，秦始皇统一了中国，创制了统一的汉字书写形式，这就是“小篆”。小篆的特点是字形平衡对称，许多汉字不仅左右对称、上下对称，一些局部也是对称的。小篆的笔画圆转，横竖均匀，粗细基本一致。

李斯《泰山刻石》

Let's Try 试一试

Re-write the following characters in small seal script.

摹写下列汉字的小篆体。

1. mountain and river 山河 (shān hé)

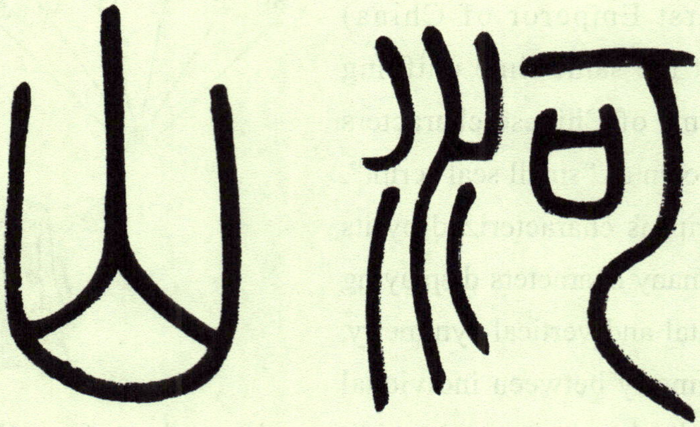

2. auspicious 吉祥 (jíxiáng)

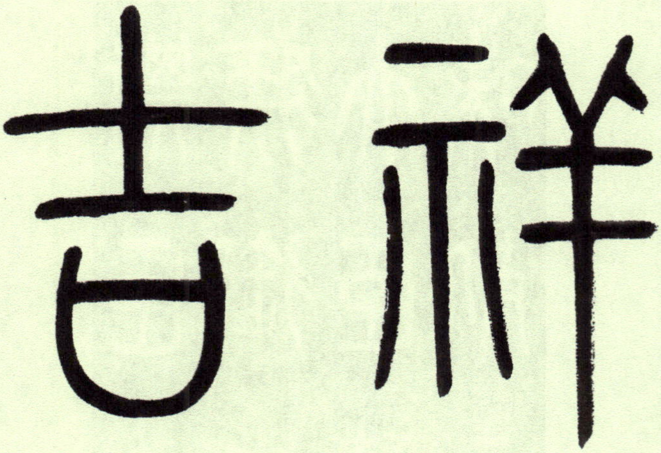

3. family harmony 家和（jiā hé）

4. virtue 厚德（hòu dé）

Clerical script 隶书

The advent of clerical script heralded the first major reform in the history of the Chinese written language. Prior to the appearance of clerical script, turtle shells, bronze items and stones were the common media used in the writing of Chinese characters. After clerical script was introduced, people started to write on pieces of wood and bamboo. Owing to the difficulty of writing characters with curved strokes on wood and bamboo, the curved characters of seal script were replaced by the straight strokes of clerical script.

隶书是汉字历史上的一次重大改革。隶书出现之前，汉字的书写载体一般是龟甲、青铜器和石头等。从隶书开始，人们把字写在竹片和木片上。在木片和竹片上写字很难写出圆转的笔画，因此隶书将篆书圆转的笔画改为方折。

◢《张迁表》

Clerical characters are symmetrical and regular in composition and the strokes are of equal distance. The ends of a number of strokes (such as the left and right falling strokes) are flicked upwards, combining to give the characters more of the artistic beauty associated with calligraphy.

隶书的结构和线条对称工整，笔画平行等距。在隶书中，撇、捺等笔画向上挑起，更具有书法的艺术美。

Chinese Learning 汉语加油站

Chinese characters have a number of basic strokes. Learning calligraphy requires to follow these specific brush motions in order to be able to write properly.
汉字有几种基本笔画。学习书法要按照运笔方法进行书写。

横
héng
Horizontal stroke

竖
shù
Vertical stroke

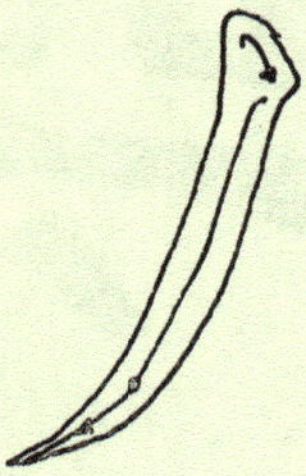

撇
piě
Left-falling stroke

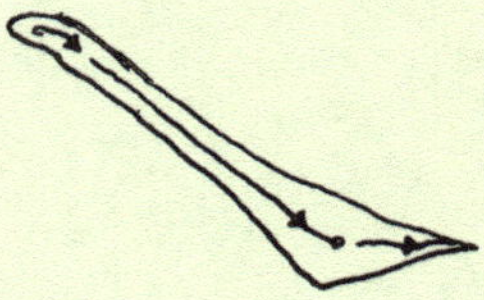

捺
nà
Right-falling stroke

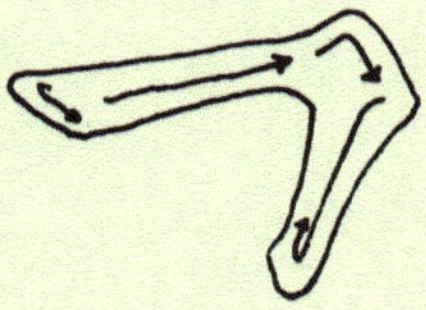

折
zhé
Turning stroke

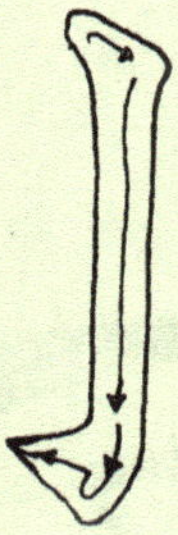

勾
gōu
Hook stroke

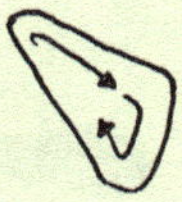

点
diǎn
Dot stroke

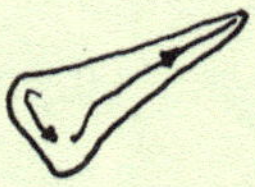

挑
tiǎo
Rising stroke

Let's Try 试一试

Re-write the following characters in clerical script.

摹写下列汉字的隶书体。

1. happiness 乐 (lè)

2. blessing 福 (fú)

3. dragon 龙 (lóng)

4. love 爱 (ài)

Regular script 楷书

Regular script is the standard by which modern Chinese handwritten characters are measured. The strokes used in Chinese characters were perfected during the period in which regular script was developed.

楷书是现代汉字手写体的参考标准，汉字的笔画在楷书阶段得以完备。

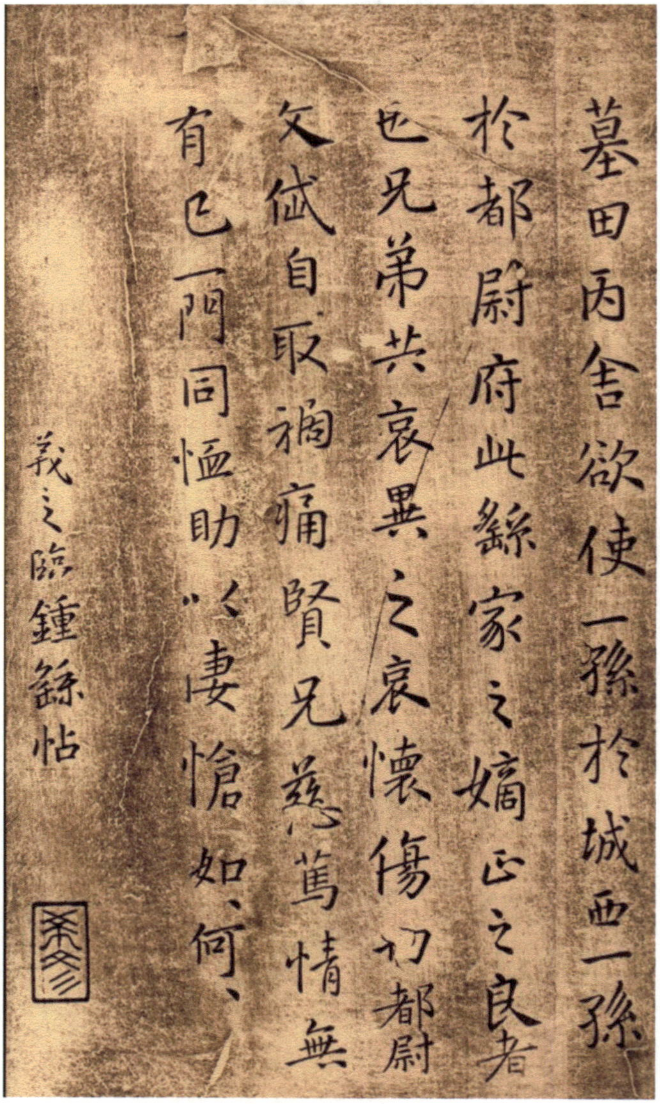

◢ 王羲之《王羲之临钟繇帖》

A Short Story about Chinese Characters 汉字小故事

It is said that the great calligraphy master of the Eastern Jin Dynasty, Wang Xizhi spent several years just practicing how to write the character *yong* 永 (eternity). He believed that *yong* was the key to mastering regular script, and that if he could write that character well, he would be able to write any character well.

相传，东晋大书法家王羲之用几年的时间专门练写“永”字。他认为，“永”字是写好楷书的关键，写好这个字，所有的字都能写好。

Legend has it that Wang Xizhi would spend hours tirelessly copying characters out again and again, all day long. One day, he was practicing deep into the night until finally he slumped down on the table and fell asleep. At that moment, a sudden gust of wind blew a white cloud into sight. Sitting on the white cloud was an old man with white hair who laughed at Wang Xizhi and said, “I'll tell you the secret to practicing calligraphy. Hold out your hand.” Wang Xizhi held out his hand doubtfully as instructed. The old man proceeded to write a character on his palm, at which the old man promptly vanished. After he had disappeared, Wang Xizhi peered down at his palm to discover the character *yong*. After thinking about this all night, he eventually realized that the character *yong* contains all six basic strokes in Chinese calligraphy. The strokes and structure of Chinese characters are encapsulated in this one character, meaning that *yong* really does contain the key to mastering Chinese calligraphy.

关于王羲之和“永”字有一个传说。据传，王羲之每天不知疲倦地练字。有一天深夜，他练着练着，竟然趴在桌上睡着了。这时，忽然刮来一阵清风，一朵白云飘然而至，云朵上有一位白发老人，笑呵呵地看着他说：“我教你一个练习书法的秘诀吧。你把手伸过来。”王羲之将信将疑地把手伸过去。老人在他手心上写了一个字。写完他就消失了。老人走后，王羲之一看手心，原来是个“永”字。他想了一整夜，终于明白了，“永”字的笔画包含“点、横、竖、勾、撇、捺”，方块字笔画和结构的诀窍都体现在这个字上了。

Let's Try 试一试

Re-write the following characters in regular script.

摹写下列汉字的楷体。

1. smile often 笑口常开（xiào kǒu cháng kāi）

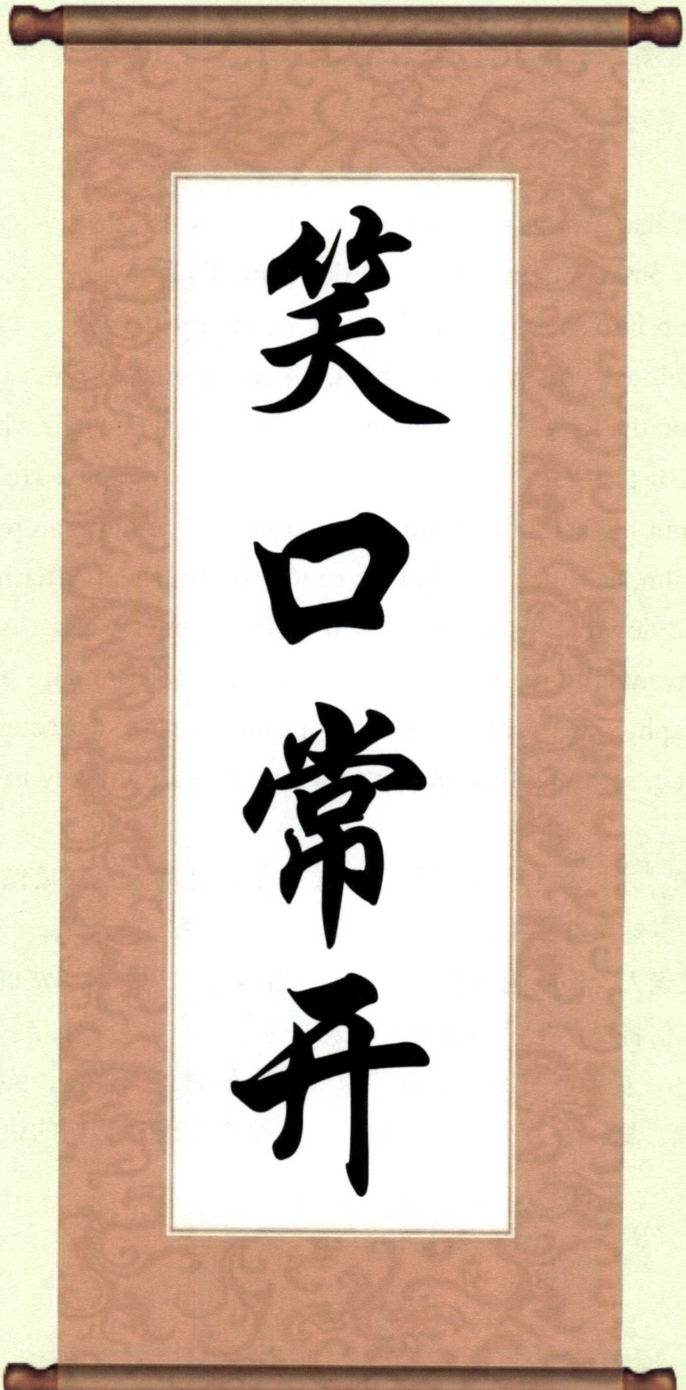

2. travel ten thousand miles 行万里路（xíng wàn lǐ lù）

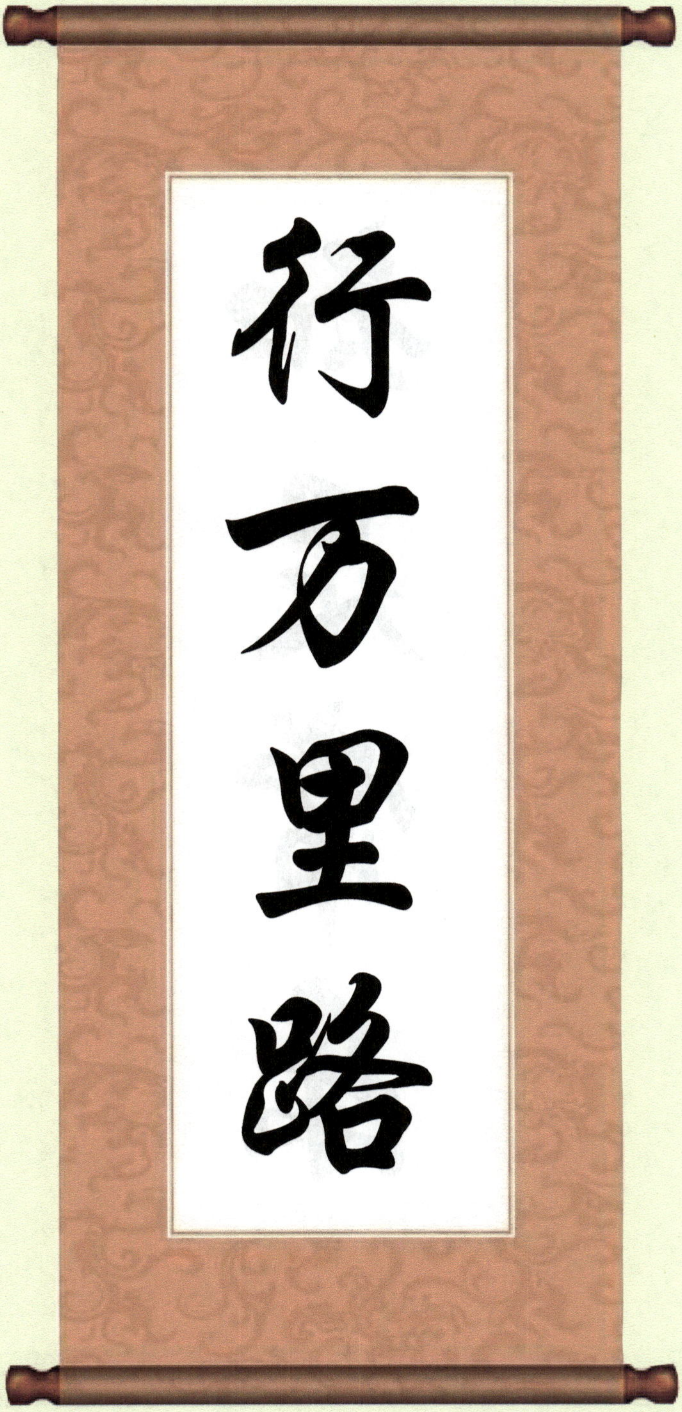

3. contentment is happiness 知足常乐（zhīzú cháng lè）

Ink Painting
水墨画

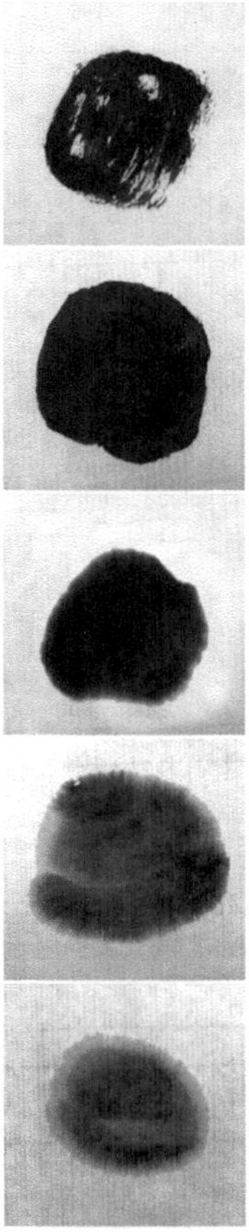

Ink painting is regarded as the traditional Chinese way of painting. As far as this form of painting is concerned, "ink (which is traditionally always black) is colour", with the shade of the "colour" varying according to how much water is added. Unlike Western oil painting, Chinese ink painting does not strive to create a realistic representation of an object, as it is not concerned with imitation, but rather with capturing the sublime beauty found in between "likeness and unlikeness."

水墨画被称为中国传统绘画。对水墨画来说，“墨即是色”，墨汁里加水的多少，颜色的深浅就随之不同。和西方油画不同的是，中国水墨画不追求对事物的真实再现，不注重摹仿，而是讲究“似与不似之间”的神韵。

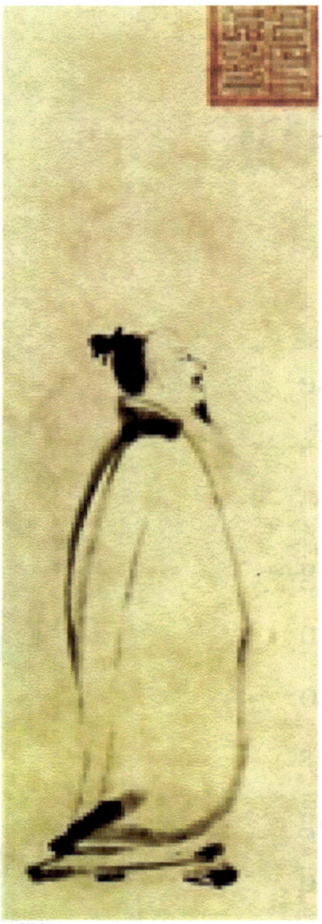

◢ 梁楷《李白行吟图》

◢ 齐白石《小鸡》

◢ 齐白石《鸟》

◢ 朱耷《鱼》

◢ 朱耷《鸟》

Let's Try 试一试

Try to mix the water and ink in different proportions to create the different shades shown in the picture below.
试着调配水和墨的比例，画出下面几种颜色。

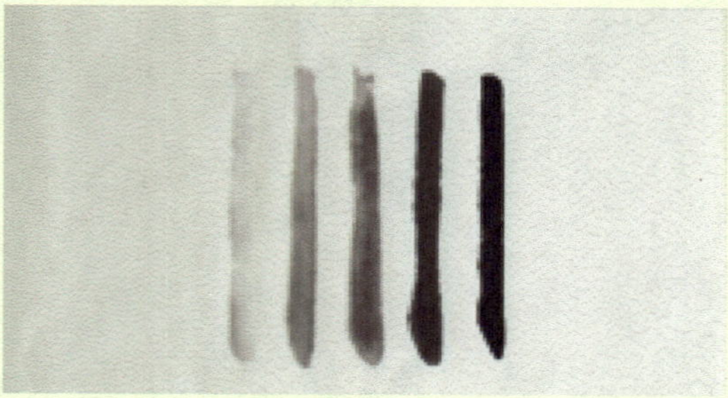

Paint Your Grapes 画葡萄

1	2	3
4	5	6

Paint Your Little Fish 画小鱼

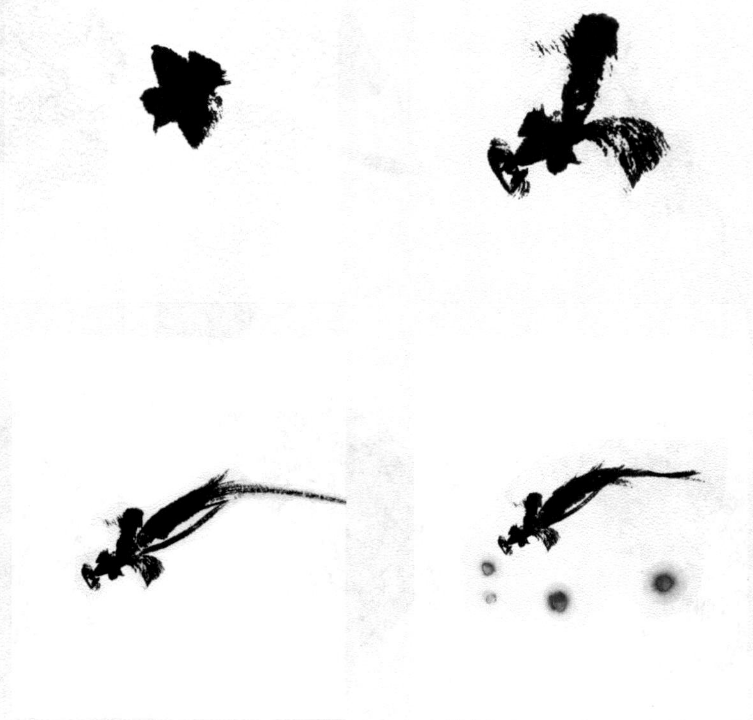

1	2
3	4

Paint Your Chrysanthemum Flower 画菊花

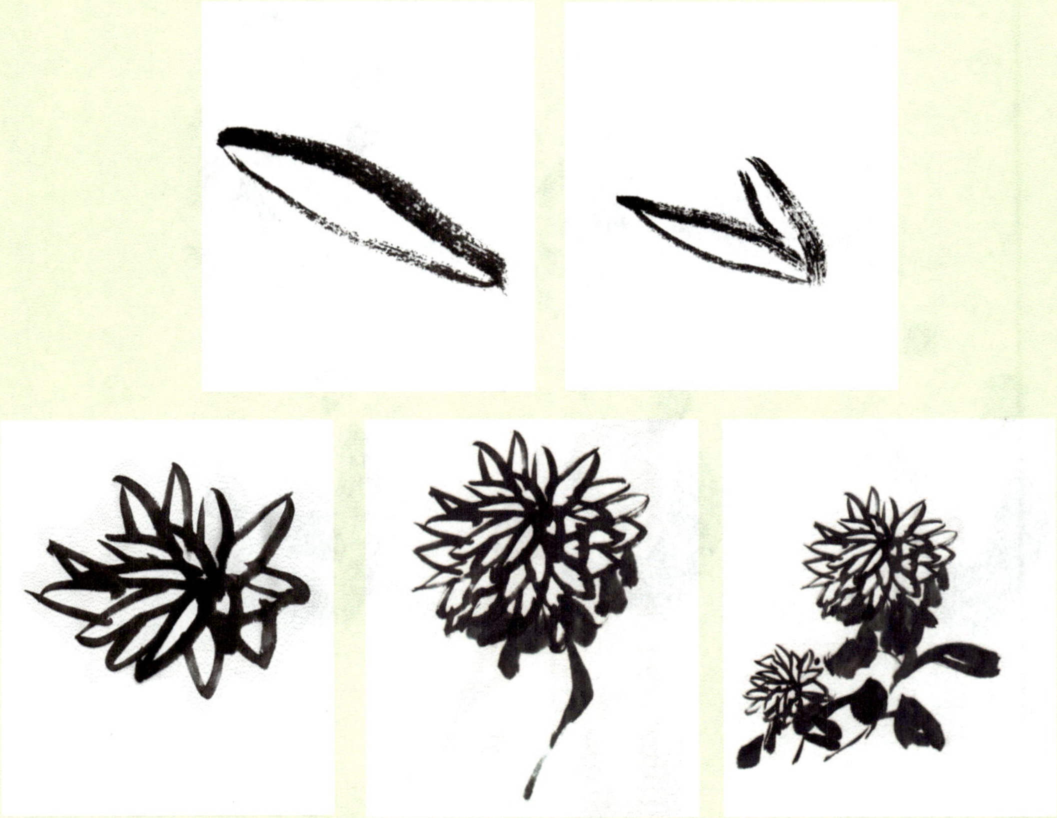

1 | 2
3 | 4 | 5

Paint Your Panda 画大熊猫

1	*2*	*3*
4	*5*	*6*

读者意见反馈

为收集对教材的意见建议，进一步完善教材编写并做好服务工作，读者可将对本教材的意见建议通过如下渠道反馈至我社。

咨询电话　400-810-0598

反馈邮箱　wy_dzyj@pub.hep.cn

通信地址　北京市朝阳区惠新东街4号富盛大厦1座
高等教育出版社总编辑办公室

邮政编码　100029

图书在版编目（CIP）数据

中国欢迎你．学书法·水墨画 / 孔子学院总部 / 国家汉办编著．-- 2 版（修订本）．-- 北京：高等教育出版社，2016.6（2023.9重印）
“中国欢迎你”短期汉语系列教材
ISBN 978-7-04-044982-2

Ⅰ．①中… Ⅱ．①孔… Ⅲ．①汉语－对外汉语教学－教材 Ⅳ．①H195.4

中国版本图书馆 CIP 数据核字（2016）第 070982 号

策划编辑	鞠 慧	责任编辑	鞠 慧 杨 曦	封面设计	乔 剑	版式设计	三月天地
书法创作	孙秀杰	水墨画创作	那泽汗	英文审译	Simon Golding	插图选配	杨 曦
责任校对	杨 曦	责任印制	耿 轩				

出版发行	高等教育出版社	网 址	http://www.hep.edu.cn
社 址	北京市西城区德外大街4号		http://www.hep.com.cn
邮政编码	100120	网上订购	http://www.hepmall.com.cn
印 刷	河北信瑞彩印刷有限公司		http://www.hepmall.com
开 本	787 mm×1092 mm 1/16		http://www.hepmall.cn
印 张	2	版 次	2011年6月第1版
字 数	50千字		2016年6月第2版
购书热线	010-58581118	印 次	2023年9月第4次印刷
咨询电话	400-810-0598	定 价	16.80 元

物 料 号 44982-00